Twenty-One Texas Heroes

A Celebration of the Lone Star State

by Eileen Santangelo Hult

Houston
2020

Copyright © 2020 by Eileen Santangelo Hult

All rights reserved. This book or any portion thereof may not be reproduced or used in any manner or media whatsoever without the permission of the publisher or author except for the use of brief quotations in a book review or academic essay.

Brighten Press edition – 2020
Friesen Press edition – 2013

ISBN 978-1-7335380-5-3 (ebook)
ISBN 978-1-7335380-4-6 (paperback)
ISBN 978-1-7335380-6-0 (hardcover)

Brighten Press
Houston, Texas

info@brightenpress.com
www.brightenpress.com

TWENTY-ONE TEXAS HEROES

A CELEBRATION OF THE LONE STAR STATE

*Dedicated to my grandmother Mary Canzoneri Rao,
born in Houston, Texas on August 27, 1894,
and to my father Congressman Alfred Santangelo
and my mother Betty Santangelo,
my heroes.*

*I want to thank my husband Gene Hult,
my sons Gene, Fred, and Rob Hult,
my sisters Betty and Patricia Santangelo,
and my brother Charles Santangelo,
for their support.*

Table of Contents

Davy Crockett (1786-1836)	1
Stephen Fuller Austin (1793-1836)	3
Sam Houston (1793-1863)	5
James Bowie (1796-1836)	7
Jane Herbert Wilkinson Long (1798-1880)	9
William Barret Travis (1809-1836)	11
Susanna Dickinson (1814-1883)	13
Ima Hogg (1882-1975)	15
Chester William Nimitz (1885-1966)	17
Samuel Taliaferro Rayburn (1882-1961)	19
Lyndon Baines Johnson (1908-1973)	21
Lynn Nolan Ryan, Jr. (1947-)	23
George Herbert Walker Bush (1924-2018)	25
Audie Leon Murphy (1924-1971)	27
George Walker Bush (1946-)	29
Willie Nelson (1933-)	31
Barbara Jordan (1936-1996)	33
Babe Didrikson Zaharias (1911-1956)	35
Charles Hardin Holley (Buddy Holly) (1936-1959)	37
Sheryl Swoopes (1971-)	39
Selena Quintanilla Perez (1971-1995)	41
About the Author	43
Image Credits	44

DAVY CROCKETT

Born in 1786 in East Tennessee,
Davy Crockett left a lasting legacy.
He became a member of the U.S. Congress.
His life ahead was filled with promise.

Crockett went to help the Texans fight.
A War of Independence was in sight.
Dressed in a hunting suit and a coonskin hat,
He left for Nacogdoches to engage in combat.

In February of 1836, he reached San Antonio.
He arrived at the fortress known as the Alamo.
Santa Anna and his army scaled the fort.
One hundred eighty Texans died in support.

Davy Crockett battled and tried to defend.
The Texans struggled and fought to the end.
On March 6, 1836, Davy Crockett was left to die.
"Remember the Alamo" became their battle cry.

The *Crockett* episodes on Disney were aired.
The impressive story of his life was shared.
"The Ballad of Davy Crockett" was sung.
Our Texas hero became our "favorite son."

Stephen Fuller Austin

Stephen Austin was a founding father of our state.
Though born in Virginia, he made Texas great.
His father's enterprise in Texas was left undone.
So he continued the legacy his father had begun.

The Austin Colony he sought to create,
The rise of Texas, the Lone Star State.
The "Old Three Hundred" were granted land.
A unique settlement was what he planned.

Mexico declared its independence from Spain.
They changed the rules for the Texas domain.
So for twenty-eight months Austin was jailed,
But his pledge to Texas was not curtailed.

After the Battle of Jacinto was won,
The Republic of Texas was begun.
In 1836, when he was forty-three,
Austin ran for the Republic's presidency.

Houston and he were on the slate.
Austin lost but became secretary of state.
In that same year, our hero died.
He was a major figure in Texas pride.

SAM HOUSTON

Sam Houston was born in Virginia in 1793.
He was a hero of Texas and a trustee.
He became a lawyer and passed the bar.
This Tennessee congressman was a star.

It was Texas where he wanted to go,
To fight in the Battle of San Jacinto.
The Mexican president knew of his fame.
Antonio Lopez de Santa Anna was his name.

As Commander of the army volunteers,
Sam Houston set aside his fears.
A declaration of Texas independence
Gave cause to Texans and their descendants.

After Santa Anna held his position,
And after the defeat at the Alamo mission,
Houston gathered his troops to fight
And set up near the Brazos River site.

After the Battle of San Jacinto was fought,
The Treaty of Velasco was sought.
The Texans won their revolution
And framed a lasting constitution.

Houston was elected the president,
The first senator and governor resident.
With his heroism, he set us straight.
He helped to make the Lone Star State.

JAMES BOWIE

Jim Bowie was a soldier and a pioneer,
A legendary figure in the wild frontier.
He learned to use a rifle and his knife.
Ursula De Veramendi became his wife.

Bowie moved to Texas, a Mexican state.
Bowie was adventurous, a daring trait.
The Bowie knife became well known.
His inspiring leadership was often shown.

He fought hostile Indians in San Antonio.
And became a leading citizen of Mexico.
When Santa Anna changed the laws,
The Texas Revolution became his cause.

In January 1836, Bowie went to San Antonio,
And fought in the Battle of the Alamo.
Santa Anna demanded surrender.
Bowie became a staunch defender.

Bowie fell ill with an unnamed disease.
The enemy soldiers would not be appeased.
On March 6, 1836, the Alamo was lost.
The hopes of the Texans had been tossed.

Jim Bowie was killed in his bed
While hostile soldiers were shot dead.
At the Alamo, a Texas hero was created.
His popularity and reputation have not faded.

JANE HERBERT WILKINSON LONG

Jane Long was a major figure in Texas tales.
Her life is filled with amazing details.
She was orphaned and had hardship in her life.
Uncle James Wilkinson saved her from strife.

She married Dr. James Long in 1815.
He'd just returned from the Battle of New Orleans.
Three children were born in this challenging time.
Their daughter Ann died in her early prime.

She lived in Bolivar while her husband fought.
In 1821, poverty struck and she was distraught.
Her third child was born on the island that year.
She was the first Anglo child in Texas to appear.

Although her husband died in 1822,
Jane was enterprising and pulled through.
She had boarding houses and a plantation.
Jane raised cattle and cotton with dedication.

We claim Jane Long as a hero in lore.
Remembered now and forever more.
She died at the age of eighty-two,
"The Mother of Texas" tried and true.

William Barret Travis

In South Carolina in 1809, Travis arrived.
He was the oldest of eleven, all who survived.
In Alabama, he became a legal apprentice.
He passed the bar and that was momentous.

He started the *Herald* in Alabama State.
Travis chose Rosanna Cato as his mate.
His marriage was troubled and soon ended.
When he moved to Texas, his life amended.

In 1831, he opened a law practice in Anahuac.
Mexicans and Texans were in constant attack.
Lieutenant colonel in the cavalry was his position.
Jim Bowie and he shared a joint commission.

His "Appeal from the Alamo" for auxiliary allies
Became a symbol of courage that all can surmise.
Travis never gave up throughout the strife.
He defended the fort at the expense of his life.

Travis helped in the plan for the Alamo mission.
They braced the fort and readied the ammunition.
William Travis died from a bullet in his head.
He became a Texas hero and his legend spread.

SUSANNA DICKINSON

The bravery of Susanna Dickinson was shown.
The "Heroine of the Alamo" was known.
The story of the Alamo was key.
She sacrificed for Texas to be free.

Texas was Mexican land.
The Texans wanted to take a stand.
But Santa Anna refused to yield.
The horror of the Alamo was sealed.

Susanna's husband went to war.
She followed him into Texas lore.
He died fighting at the Alamo,
A large fortress in San Antonio.

Susanna was spared and sent to go,
And told General Houston about the Alamo.
He listened to her tale of woe,
Then fought the Battle of San Jacinto.

She died at the age of sixty-eight,
The Battle of the Alamo made her great.
She was buried in Austin in 1883.
Susanna's message was her destiny.

IMA HOGG

Born in Minneola, Texas in 1882,
Ima Hogg was a Texas hero true blue.
Named the "first lady" of Texas State,
Her contributions made her great.

She helped her dad on the campaign trail.
He ran for governor and he prevailed.
She learned about political meetings,
And became adept at friendly greetings.

She studied piano from the age of three.
In NYC she attended the conservatory.
She helped to enrich the Texas culture
By starting the Houston Symphony Orchestra.

Through Bayou Bend and its antiques collection,
She contributed to Texas and showed her affection.
Her generosity was an honorable trait.
She was benevolent to the Lone Star State.

She donated Varner-Hogg Plantation,
And created the Hogg Foundation.
She died at the age of ninety-three,
Buried in Austin Oakwood Cemetery.

CHESTER WILLIAM NIMITZ

Born in Fredericksburg, Texas in 1885,
Nimitz's grandfather taught him to strive.
He graduated the Naval Academy in 1905.
On the gunboat *Panay* he did arrive.

When he ran the destroyer *Decatur* aground,
He was court-martialed and submarine bound.
After four lengthy commands on submarines,
He managed the building of diesel engine machines.

He married Catherine Freeman in 1913.
He had four children with time in between.
In World War I he was commander of a battleship,
Then went to Pearl Harbor to build the sub base strip.

He studied at Navy War College to create a war plan.
He used the war model when World War II began.
It was after Pearl Harbor's terrible defeat,
He was selected commander in-chief, Pacific Fleet.

In charge of air, land, and sea, Nimitz shifted into offensive.
They defeated the Japanese Navy in a battle quite intensive.
In the Battle of the Coral Sea, and the Battle of Midway,
His campaigns left the Japanese in total disarray.

Appointed fleet admiral by Roosevelt in December of '44,
Nimitz's victories were responsible for ending the war.
The *Missouri* in Tokyo Bay was the site of the accord.
The Japanese surrendered with Nimitz on board.

October 5, 1945 was officially designated as "Nimitz Day."
He was buried in the National Cemetery near San Francisco Bay.
Nimitz was a five-star admiral honored for his brave ways.
He was a Texas hero who deserves our respect and praise.

Samuel Taliaferro Rayburn

Born in 1882, Rayburn was from Flag Springs.
His flights of imagination gave him wings.
He attended East Texas Normal College.
Finished in two years, prepared with knowledge.

He studied law and how to legislate.
The Texas House was his entry gate.
In 1913 he went to Washington D.C.
For forty-eight years he held the political key.

From Wilson to Johnson he made his fame.
Speaker of the House was his domain.
A man of action and independence, too,
Rayburn was proved tried and true.

Rayburn helped pass the New Deal legislation.
He co-wrote the bill enacting rural electrification.
He was Lyndon B. Johnson's political mentor.
He was the American people's public defender.

The Sam Rayburn Library at Bonham stands.
It's a special tribute to this extraordinary man.
His home in Bonham was left to his foundation.
It became a museum for the whole nation.

In 1961, Rayburn became unwell.
At seventy-nine he bid us farewell.
Hospitals, schools, bases, and more
Have memorialized him in Texas lore.

LYNDON BAINES JOHNSON

Lyndon Baines Johnson, known as LBJ,
Was born in Texas around Johnson City way.
"Lady Bird" Taylor became his wife.
Her exceptional qualities enhanced his life.

A lieutenant in the Navy, a Silver Star earned,
Six times in congress he was affirmed.
He ran for the U.S. Senate with great pride.
"Lady Bird" Luck was on his side.

In 1960, he ran for vice president.
Kennedy chose him, the reasons quite evident.
In 1963, JFK was tragically shot,
So Johnson took on the presidential spot.

As president, he advocated the fight
For Black-American civil rights.
He enacted Medicare and conservation laws.
His fight on poverty was a righteous cause.

The Vietnam War was an ongoing fight.
Johnson in vain tried to set it right.
But peace was not easy to attain.
The war continued and caused great pain.

Johnson did not run in the next election,
But worked for peace in a different direction.
He died of a heart attack in 1973.
His life was dedicated to this country.

Luci and Lynda Johnson were always there,
They learned the legacy of political care.
The LBJ Library stands in Austin today.
He was the 36th president of the U.S.A.

LYNN NOLAN RYAN, JR.

Nolan Ryan's fame took flight.
Baseball was his line of sight.
Born in 1947 in Texas the state.
He played Little League, an all-star great.

In 1965, he joined the Mets.
The California Angels was the next.
He set league records as a pitcher.
With the Houston Astros he was a fixture.

His nickname was the "Ryan Express."
With the Texas Rangers he met success.
By 1991 he had pitched seven no-hitters.
His baseball team had no quitters.

In 1999 he made the Hall of Fame.
Cooperstown recorded his proper claim.
The Rangers, Astros, and the Mets
All retired his uniform sets.

He was made president of the Rangers.
He purchased the team with no strangers.
He was also made the CEO.
With Ryan's help, the Rangers would grow.

Ryan wrote a fitness guide.
Advil was his TV pride.
The Ryan Dollar was created.
Ryan's Beef is highly rated.

Dynamic Ruth Holdoff is his wife.
Ryan's three sons are in his life.
Highways and schools are named after him.
He's a Texas hero with vigor and vim.

George Herbert Walker Bush

A man of strength at his core,
George Bush was born in 1924.
He moved to West Texas to invest.
He was successful in his quest.

He joined the Navy at eighteen years of age.
World War II was another page.
The Distinguished Flying Cross was received.
Fifty-eight combat missions he achieved.

In 1945, Barbara Pierce became his wife.
They moved to New Haven to start a new life.
At Yale, he was in the Skull and Bones society.
George Bush was known for his propriety.

While in Texas, he reached common ground.
Zapata Petroleum Company he co-found.
He became president of Zapata Offshore Company,
In which oil was produced most abundantly.

He moved to Houston and was a conservative.
Became a representative. The vote was affirmative.
Bush was liaison to China, and CIA director.
Then he became a Rice University professor.

He was appointed ambassador to the United Nations.
He worked as VP on government deregulations.
In 1989, Bush became the president of the U.S.
And Pennsylvania Avenue became his address.

After four years as president of the United States,
George and Barbara moved back to home base.
Their oldest son became the U.S. president.
This was quite a profound accomplishment.

So we in Texas held them dear
When at Astros games they both appeared.
Barbara and George came as a pair.
Texas heroes, we declare.

Audie Leon Murphy

Born in Kingston, Texas in 1924,
Murphy was a hero in Texas lore.
He fought bravely in the second World War.
The Medal of Honor, we can't ignore.

His valor and courage brought him far,
Winning the distinguished Silver Star.
From private to major, he rose in the ranks.
With the Bronze Star, we gave him our thanks.

Murphy fought in Italy, Germany, and France.
He stopped the enemies in their advance.
Wounded in battle with injuries severe,
He won the prestigious French Croix de Guerre.

He came home to Texas with parades and more.
Joined the National Guard at the end of the war.
He wrote about himself and all of his strife.
To Hell and Back was a movie about his life.

His post-war syndrome was quite a fight.
His frequent nightmares kept him up at night.
He died in a tragic plane crash in 1971.
His bold and heroic life was done.

June 20th was named "Audie Murphy Day."
The Cotton Museum has his medals on display.
Highways and schools were built in his name.
He's a Texas hero of renown and fame.

George Walker Bush

In 1946, George Walker Bush arrived.
The war had ended. The nation thrived.
He grew up in Texas and loved the state.
When he met Laura, he found his mate.

He studied at Yale and Harvard schools.
Bush learned business and political rules.
He started a company that drilled for oil,
Then went to Austin to be Governor awhile.

From Austin to Washington, he moved away,
And became the 41st president of the U.S.A.
To protect our country was his prayer,
And keep us safe and free from fear.

But al-Qaeda terrorists came along.
September 11th was a frightful wrong.
Bush fought back to show our strength.
We fought two wars at great length.

He launched an initiative to combat AIDS.
His efforts in Africa were his personal crusades.
Preventative care helped millions of families.
He helped to reduce the many casualties.

Dallas is where George and Laura reside.
A touch of history they do provide.
The Bush Presidential Library was key.
It was built at Southern Methodist University.

His book *Decision Points* showed his intent
Of the judgments made while he was president.
His resolve and determination brought him praise.
George Bush is a hero in so many ways.

WILLIE NELSON

Born in Abbot, Texas in 1933,
Nelson was a singer with a banjo on his knee.
He started out at ten in a Bohemian Polka band.
Later he sang Country in a park called Opryland.

Columbia Records signed him on in '72.
His songs became hits that everyone knew.
"Blue Eyes Crying in the Rain" was great.
"Always on My Mind" was for his mate.

A red bandanna and t-shirt were his gear.
"On the Road Again" helped his career.
His guitar and banjo he always carried.
His eclectic style was very varied.

The unofficial "Mayor of Austin" was a tagged name.
He played at the Olympics—that brought him fame.
Willie toured the world with great success.
He made his home in Spicewood, Texas.

Willie is a Texas hero and legendary star.
As a prolific writer and singer he went far.
As a producer and activist he is an icon.
To the people of Texas he will always live on.

Barbara Jordan

Jordan was born in the Texas Fifth Ward.
She was loved, respected, and adored.
Her dad and grandfather were both ministers.
She learned how to orate and how to administer.

Self-sufficient, strong minded, and independent,
Ms. Jordan's life achievement was transcendent.
Her skill in oratory brought Jordan many awards.
She discovered that speaking out had its rewards.

Jordon went to Texas Southern University.
She excelled in college despite adversity.
Jordan was in many debate competitions.
And spoke about her political positions.

Jordan went to Boston University School of Law.
She excelled in her studies as never before.
Jordan qualified for the bar in Texas,
And successfully started a private law practice.

She organized black Americans in Harris County,
And helped John F. Kennedy in 1960.
Elected to the Texas House from the 11th District,
She was the first woman and second black ever picked.

She was elected to the U.S. Congress in 1972.
Her speeches on duty and Watergate were on cue.
Jordan was a star in '76 at the Democratic Convention.
She fought against crime and civil rights suspension.

She became a professor at the University of Texas.
She developed the disease of multiple sclerosis.
She won the Presidential Medal of Freedom in '94.
The Texas and National Hall of Fame was more.

She won the US Military Academy's Thayer Award.
Her contributions to Texas have endured.
She died in '96 and is buried at Texas State Cemetery.
Her deeds and achievements were highly exemplary.

Babe Didrikson Zaharias

Babe was born in Port Arthur town,
Then moved to Beaumont and all around.
Babe excelled in all kinds of sports.
She loved hurdles, golf, and tennis courts.

Named the World's Greatest Athlete,
She was part of America's sports elite.
Her name was part of Babe Ruth's fame.
Mildred was her real first name.

At sixteen she played for her company's team.
On the basketball court, she could be seen.
Competed in the National Women's track meet.
In track and field, she was hard to beat.

Not only in sports did Babe compete,
But as a seamstress she reached a feat.
In 1931, she won a sewing exhibition
In the South Texas State Fair competition.

In 1932, she went to the L.A. Olympics,
With the javelin throw, she was transfixed.
Babe won first place in the javelin throw.
She broke the world record and was set to go.

Babe won a gold and silver medal coup,
The eighty-meter hurdle and high jump too.
Later, professional golf became her game,
And gave her name some further fame.

Babe lived her life with George Zaharias,
But she died of colon cancer in 1956.
Babe was the name by which she was known.
She was a Texas hero who we can call our own.

CHARLES HARDIN HOLLEY (BUDDY HOLLY)

Born in Lubbock, Texas in 1936,
He learned to sing and write limericks.
At an early age, he won recognition
When he sang at age five in a competition.

Buddy played the acoustic guitar.
His cheery pop-rock style made him a star.
He sang "That'll Be the Day" on TV.
The Ed Sullivan Show was a guarantee.

American Bandstand was another break,
Gave him some fame and a fair shake.
"Peggy Sue" and "Oh, Boy!" went to the top.
He became a legend of American pop.

He went on tour here and abroad.
With "Maybe Baby," his records soared.
In 1959 came that fateful event.
Holly's plane crashed on ascent.

Ritchie Valens and the Bopper were killed,
Their lives and music unfulfilled.
Don McLean wrote "American Pie"
To remember "the day the music died."

The Buddy Holly Story was released.
Buddy's legend rightly increased.
Through groups like the Beatles and the Grateful Dead,
Buddy's music influence was widely spread.

Our Texas hero is held in esteem.
The Crickets were part of his music team.
Lubbock has made him a champion of song.
His memory and music are forever strong.

SHERYL SWOOPES

Sheryl Swoopes is a basketball star.
Her expertise brought her far.
Brownfield, Texas was where she began.
To be tops in her sport was her game plan.

From South Plains Junior to Texas Tech College,
She achieved credits and much knowledge.
An NCAA championship was her gain.
As a female champion Sheryl reigned.

In 1993, in the NCAA Final-Four game,
She led her team to championship fame.
Forty-seven points in one game scored.
She also won the noted Naismith Award.

The Houston Comets brought her more.
She became a star in basketball lore.
The prestigious gold medal was supreme,
When she played for the U.S. Olympic Team.

Air Swoopes became a Nike shoe
As her fame and fortune rose and grew.
Most Valuable Player was a fantasy trip.
Her team won the WNBA championship.

So Swoopes is a Texas hero acclaimed,
The pride of women's sports proclaimed.
Her Olympic medals can all be framed.
A lasting legacy she obtained.

SELENA QUINTANILLA PEREZ

Born in Lake Jackson in 1971.
Her Latin songs became a home run.
She married bandleader Chris Perez in 1992.
He played in Selena's band with a great review.

At nineteen, her album *Ven Commigo* went gold,
the first female Tejana artist to reach in that fold.
Then Yolanda Saldivar started a fan club,
And headed Selena's retail clothes hub.

Selena Live won a Grammy award.
The album *Amor Prohibido* soared.
It was Mexican-American Album of the year.
Selena's career was in high gear.

Her album *Dreaming of You* was unencumbered,
Making number one on the U.S. Billboard 200.
Songs like "I Could Fall in Love" made it big.
Selena's Latin America tour was a successful gig.

She visited schools to stress education.
She donated her time to civic organizations.
Then on that very fateful day,
Yolanda Saldivar shot Selena away.

George W. Bush created April 16th as "Selena Day."
Thousands of fans came to mourn her passing away.
The U.S. Postal Service's "Latin Legends" honored Selena.
She was a Texas hero in the music arena.

About the Author

EILEEN SANTANGELO HULT is a teacher with twenty-five years of experience. Mrs. Hult taught for twelve years in Clear Creek ISD, League City, TX, and as an adjunct at University of Houston Clear Lake. She was cited in *Who's Who Among American Teachers* in 2005. She has an M.B.A and an M.S. in Education. In 2007, she received the Marian and Speros Martel Early Childhood Educator of the Year Award from the Children's Museum of Houston. Her husband Gene passed away in 2020. Mrs. Hult lives in Clear Lake City, Houston. Her grandmother's love of Texas prompted her to write this book on Texas heroes.

IMAGE CREDITS

Page 1: Davy Crockett
Credit: YANGCHAO/Shutterstock.com

Page 3: Stephen Fuller Austin
Angela Orlando, DRT, 6th Generation Texan
Credit: Native Houstonian/Flickr

Page 5: Sam Houston
Credit: John Kropewnicki/Shutterstock.com

Page 7: James Bowie
Credit: Boston, Barclay Gibson Photography

Page 9: Jane Herbert Wilkinson Long
Credit: A composite effort by the Bolivar Peninsula Cultural Foundation

Page 11: William Barret Travis
Statue of William Travis, Texas Hall, Dallas
Credit: Barclay Gibson Photography

Page 13: Susanna Dickinson
Credit: Image by Artist, Mark Barnett

Page 15: Ima Hogg
Credit: Wikimedia Commons, Public Domain, website/mfah.org

Page 17: Chester William Nimitz
Credit: nadi555/Shutterstock.com

Page 19: Samuel Taliaferro Rayburn
Alfred E. Santangelo being sworn into the U.S. House of Representatives by Sam Rayburn, January 1957. From left, Eileen Santangelo Hult, Mary Jo Santangelo Nocero, Alfred E. Santangelo, Sam Rayburn, Georgia Santangelo, Betty L. Santangelo, Mary Rao.
Credit: Dev O'Neil

Page 21: Lyndon Baines Johnson
Credit: Public Domain/lbjlibrary.net

Page 23: Lynn Nolan Ryan, Jr.
Credit: Pitcher Nolan Ryan/Dreamstime.com

Page 25: George Herbert Walker Bush
Credit: Wikimedia Commons, White House, Public Domain

Page 27: Audie Leon Murphy
Credit: Chris Vaughn/Shutterstock.com

Page 29: George Walker Bush
Credit: White House, Public Domain

Page 31: Willie Nelson
Credit: Christopher Halloran/Shutterstock.com

Page 33: Barbara Jordan
Credit: Statue of Barbara Jordan at Austin, #68818719 Pixmac

Page 35: Babe Didrikson Zaharias
Credit: Neftali/Shutterstock.com

Page 37: Charles Hardin Holley (Buddy Holly)
Credit: RoidRanger/Shutterstock.com

Page 39: Sheryl Swoopes
Personal appearance, July 11, 2008, Carter Subaru
Credit: Seattle Storm, rks-seattle's photostream

Page 41: Selena Quintanilla-Perez
Selena at 1991 Tejano Music Awards in San Antonio, Texas
Credit: Wikipedia Commons, Photographer, Mfd79/creativecommons.org

*The Power of Words to
Enlighten and Entertain*

With all the many other demands on your attention in the world, we appreciate you taking the time to read this book.

We welcome you to explore our growing list of poetry, humor, and children's book titles at **brightenpress.com**.